while *they* *are* sleeping

while *they* are sleeping

12 character traits *to* pray *for* the children you love

anne arkins & gary harrell

FamilyLife Publishing®
Little Rock, Arkansas

WHILE THEY ARE SLEEPING: 12 CHARACTER TRAITS TO PRAY FOR THE CHILDREN YOU LOVE
FamilyLife Publishing®
5800 Ranch Drive
Little Rock, Arkansas 72223
1-800-FL-TODAY • FamilyLife.com
FLTI, d/b/a FamilyLife®, is a ministry of Campus Crusade for Christ International®

ISBN: 978-1-60200-396-5

Design: Brand Navigation, LLC

Cover image: Copyright © Veer, a Corbis Corporation Brand/Yarruta

Printed in the United States of America
16 15 14 13 12   2 3 4 5 6

FAMILYLIFE®
Help for today. Hope for tomorrow.

contents

foreword vii

how to use this
    prayer guide 1

kindness 3

humility 11

teachability 19

forgiveness 27

obedience 35

discernment 43

purity 51

responsibility 59

courage 67

servanthood 75

contentment 83

endurance 91

appendix:
    character-building
    suggestions 99

foreword

Abraham Lincoln wrote, "I have been driven many times to my knees by the overwhelming conviction that I had nowhere else to go." As a parent of six children, I can relate. Countless times I've felt compelled to pray because of my own shortcomings as a mom. Like Lincoln, I've also been driven to pray for wisdom in the training issues my husband, Dennis, and I have encountered with each of our children and the circumstances they face in life.

Prayer is essential to parenting. As parents, we can seek God not just in those desperate moments when we feel clueless about what to do, but in a proactive way as we ask for His hand to work in our children's hearts, forming their character, developing beneficial attributes, and molding each child's will to follow Him. Prayer pulls us into sync with the rhythm of God's purposes for our families. And there's no better way to pray in harmony with His will than to use the very words of the Scripture.

I'm delighted to introduce this little book to you. You'll enjoy the perspective it brings and the unique way it aligns the concerns and dreams we have for our children with scripturally based prayers that we can pray over them *while they are sleeping*. There is nothing like a peacefully sleeping child, even when that child is a teen! Take advantage of those moments of calm in your home and invite God to be at work, accomplishing His will in each child he has entrusted to you.

Yours for the next generation of children who will become messengers of truth to those who will follow. May they be strong and mighty for God's kingdom.

Barbara Rainey

how to use
this prayer guide

God shapes the world by prayer.
—E. M. Bounds

The *While They Are Sleeping* prayer guide is organized into twelve sections highlighting different character traits to pray for and nurture in your child. You can pray through all twelve character traits in the order presented, or you can pray through them in any order you choose.

Five days have been devoted to each character trait, and each day's meditation includes scripture passages relating to the trait in focus, as well as prayers to pray for your child. You can pray through the daily prayers all at once during your devotional time or throughout the day.

Personal Prayer sections will help you consider a character trait as it uniquely applies to your child and his or her circumstances. (To ensure gender-inclusive language, we've alternated gender pronouns in the prayers from day to day.)

At the end of each section, you'll find character-related tips:

- You-and-Me Time: for connecting with your child or children
- Live It Out: innovative ways you can practically develop a trait together

As you pray, God may impress upon you life-application steps more specific to your child. Consider recording those steps on the Observations, Prayers, and Answers page at the end of each section.

Additionally, use the prayer-journal page (Observations, Prayers, and Answers) to record current circumstances, feelings, specific prayers concerning your child, and answers to prayer as you witness them!

It's our prayer for you and your family that God will use this time with Him to accomplish "immeasurably more than all we ask or imagine, according to his power that is at work within us" (Eph. 3:20 NIV)—for this generation and those yet to be born.

> *Arise, cry out in the night, as the watches of the night begin;*
> *pour out your heart like water in the presence of the Lord.*
> *Lift up your hands to him for the lives of your children.*
> —LAMENTATIONS 2:19 (NIV)

kindness

THOUGHTFULNESS
ARISING *from* LOVE

The power of prayer is in the One who
hears it and not the one who says it.
Our prayers do make a difference.

—MAX LUCADO

kindness DAY ONE

"[The good Samaritan] went to [the injured man] and bandaged his wounds, pouring on oil and wine. Then he put the man on his own donkey, took him to an inn and took care of him. The next day he took out two silver coins and gave them to the innkeeper. 'Look after him,' he said, 'and when I return, I will reimburse you for any extra expense you may have.'"

—LUKE 10:34–35 (NIV)

PRAYER FOCUS

Father, may _____ be willing to give of herself to help a person in need. May _____ not only see the needs of others but act upon those needs in a sacrificial way. Deliver _____ from holding too tightly to her possessions. Give her a willingness to share her resources with others.

This is how we know what love is: Jesus Christ laid down his life for us. And we ought to lay down our lives for our brothers. If anyone has material possessions and sees his brother in need but has no pity on him, how can the love of God be in him? Dear children, let us not love with words or tongue but with actions and in truth.
—1 JOHN 3:16-18 (NIV)

PRAYER FOCUS

Gracious Father, open _____'s heart to know the real love of Jesus' gift of salvation. Help her to be willing to give of herself as He did. May _____ be sensitive to see ways she can meet the needs of the people around her. Father, help _____ to love others not only "with words or tongue but with actions and in truth."

*Kindness is giving up something
for the benefit of another.*

kindness DAY TWO

He who despises his neighbor sins,
but blessed is he who is kind to the needy.
—PROVERBS 14:21 (NIV)

PRAYER FOCUS

Father, as _____ sees those around him in need (whether that need is physical, emotional, or spiritual), may his heart be touched. Give him a desire to help them. May _____ realize that it is a sin to hate his neighbor, but being kind to those in need will please You and bring blessing.

[Remember] the words the Lord Jesus himself said: "It is more blessed to give than to receive." —ACTS 20:35 (NIV)

PRAYER FOCUS

Lord Jesus, may _____ recognize the value of being kind. I pray that _____ will experience the blessing that comes with giving.

A gentle answer turns away wrath, but a harsh word stirs up anger. —PROVERBS 15:1 (NIV)

PRAYER FOCUS

Gentle Father, cause _____ to learn to respond to the anger of another with a gentle answer. Open the eyes of _____ to see that gentleness and kindness of speech can do far more than an unkind word to turn away another person's anger.

Kindness is having a sensitive
spirit toward others.

kindness DAY THREE

*"'When a stranger resides with you in your land, you shall
not do him wrong. The stranger who resides with you shall be to
you as the native among you, and you shall love him as yourself,
for you were aliens in the land of Egypt: I am the LORD your God.'"*
—LEVITICUS 19:33–34 (NASB)

PRAYER FOCUS

Loving Father, as _____ comes in contact with new people in her
life, may she treat them as she would a friend. Help _____ to love,
accept, and show compassion for the people she encounters.

"Treat others the same way you want them to treat you." —LUKE 6:31 (NASB)

PRAYER FOCUS

Lord, develop in _____ a willingness to treat others as she would like
others to treat her.

*"I was hungry and you gave me something to eat, I was thirsty and you gave me some-
thing to drink, I was a stranger and you invited me in, I needed clothes and you
clothed me, I was sick and you looked after me, I was in prison and you came to visit
me."* —MATTHEW 25:35–36 (NIV)

PRAYER FOCUS

Lord Jesus, I pray that _____ would learn to look at the needs of
others with mercy and tenderness. Encourage _____ to become a
lifeline to those around her in practical ways that meet their true needs.

*Kindness is treating others the way
we would like to be treated.*

kindness DAY FOUR

Get rid of all bitterness, rage and anger, brawling and slander,
along with every form of malice. Be kind and compassionate to
one another, forgiving each other, just as in Christ God forgave you.
—EPHESIANS 4:31–32 (NIV)

PRAYER FOCUS

Loving, gracious Father, help _____ to resolve his conflicts in ways
that honor You, instead of harboring bitterness or anger in his heart. May he
never shout angrily or say things to hurt others. I pray that _____
would not do evil things but would be kind and loving. Give _____
the desire to forgive just as You have forgiven him in Christ, laying down Your
life when he was Your enemy.

Joseph said to [his brothers], "Don't be afraid. Am I in the place of God? You intended
to harm me, but God intended it for good to accomplish what is now being done, the
saving of many lives. So then, don't be afraid. I will provide for you and your children."
And he reassured them and spoke kindly to them. —GENESIS 50:19–21 (NIV)

PRAYER FOCUS

Father, I pray that _____ might become sensitive to Your control of
the events and people in his life. Show _____, like Joseph, how to
handle the negative thoughts he has toward others, especially those who have
caused him pain or offended him.

PERSONAL PRAYER

Pray for your child in specific areas where he is encountering opportunities to
extend undeserved kindness.

Kindness is controlling our negative
thoughts toward others.

kindness DAY FIVE

[In the last days,] people will love only themselves and their money; they will be proud and boastful, sneering at God, disobedient to their parents, ungrateful to them, and thoroughly bad. They will be hardheaded and never give in to others.
—2 TIMOTHY 3:2–3 (TLB)

PRAYER FOCUS

O Lord, guard the heart of my child from the error of selfishness. I earnestly pray that _____ would not be caught up in thinking only of herself and her needs. Keep _____ from being proud and boastful, disregarding You, disobeying those You've placed in authority over her, and being ungrateful. Cause _____ to recognize selfishness in her life and confess it to You, exchanging it for kindness.

"Everyone who exalts himself will be humbled, and he who humbles himself will be exalted." —LUKE 14:11 (NASB)

PRAYER FOCUS

Father, deliver _____ from any attitude of self-exaltation. Grant a willingness and eagerness to be humble before You and others. Refocus the vision of _____'s selfishness so that she can see the needs of others and discern what's best for them.

PERSONAL PRAYER

Pray for protection, awareness, and deliverance from specific temptations your child is facing with selfishness and pride.

Selfishness attends only to one's own needs and interests; kindness acts with regard for the needs and interests of others.

you *and* me time

1. Read together age-appropriate portions of the Old Testament account of Joseph (especially chapters 37 and 42–45) using your family's favorite Bible storybook. Ask your child to relate his or her thoughts about how Joseph responded to his brothers. Help your child see how the character trait of kindness ultimately reflected Joseph's faith in God's control, not in other people. To take the concept a step further, have school-age children act out the story.
2. Read Matthew 6:2–4 together. Plan a "secret kindness mission" with your child to bless other family members, neighbors, or friends. Have fun devising a sneaky way to show someone kindness without that person discovering the plan in advance, or possibly its source.
3. Draw a name at each mealtime this week, and take turns around the table encouraging the selected family member with kind words.

live *it* out

1. When one of your children is having a bad day, make a plan with another child to graciously cheer him or her up in a way personally meaningful to the sibling—such as bringing a brooding adolescent a plate of his or her favorite cookies or a favorite drink.
2. Ask family members to consider what they might give up this week that would benefit someone else with a need. Help them think outside the box as they realize the needs of others and evaluate what resources they have available to meet those needs (e.g., time, the ability to do physical labor, a reputation with friends). Discuss, too, how at times the unkindness of others can be a signal of what they truly need— even though they're communicating that need in an unpleasant way. At the end of the week, share your experiences of sacrificing for others.

kindness

OBSERVATIONS, PRAYERS, AND ANSWERS

_____

_____

_____

_____

_____

_____

_____

_____

_____

_____

_____

_____

_____

_____

_____

_____

_____

_____

_____

humility

SEEING OURSELVES *as* GOD SEES *us*— *no* GREATER, *no* LESS

The greatest thing anyone can
do for God and man is pray.

—S. D. GORDON

humility DAY ONE

Do nothing out of selfish ambition or vain conceit, but in humility
consider others better than yourselves. Each of you should look
not only to your own interests, but also to the interests of others.
—Philippians 2:3–4 (NIV)

PRAYER FOCUS

Merciful God, You allowed Your only Son to humble Himself and become our
servant. He did nothing out of selfish ambition or self-importance. May
_____ likewise humbly consider others before himself. Give
_____ the sensitivity to see beyond his own interests to what is
important for those around him.

Be devoted to one another in brotherly love. Honor one another above yourselves.
—Romans 12:10 (NIV)

PRAYER FOCUS

O Lord, develop in _____ a genuine willingness to become devoted
to others in brotherly love. Liberate _____ to see the importance of
putting others before himself in his life.

PERSONAL PRAYER

Pray for your child's repentance in specific areas of his life where he's tempted by
self-importance or selfish ambition.

Humility is thinking more highly
of others than self.

humility DAY TWO

"The greatest among you will be your servant.
For whoever exalts himself will be humbled,
and whoever humbles himself will be exalted."
—MATTHEW 23:11-12 (NIV)

PRAYER FOCUS

Lord, it's a hard thing to learn how to put others above yourself and serve them with a willing heart in true humility. Create in _____'s heart a recep-tiveness to the opportunities in her life that help her to apply this principle. Reveal to _____ that real character is being able to humble herself before you and others.

"You are not to be like [those who lord it over others]. Instead, the greatest among you should be like the youngest, and the one who rules like the one who serves."
—LUKE 22:26 (NIV)

PRAYER FOCUS

Father, allow _____ to catch a vision of what Christ meant when He said that the "greatest among you should be like the youngest, and the one who rules like the one who serves." May she desire to develop this attitude in her life and recognize ways she can grow in this area.

PERSONAL PRAYER

Pray that your child will learn humility as she serves others.

Humility is developing spiritual greatness
through serving others.

humility DAY THREE

The high and lofty one who inhabits eternity, the Holy One, says
this: I live in that high and holy place where those with contrite,
humble spirits dwell; and I refresh the humble and give new
courage to those with repentant hearts.

—ISAIAH 57:15 (TLB)

PRAYER FOCUS

Lord God, You alone are the high and lofty One. Give _____ a
humble attitude before You. May he have a repentant spirit and be receptive to
Your Spirit dwelling in him.

Scripture says: "God opposes the proud but gives grace to the humble." . . . Humble
yourselves before the Lord, and he will lift you up. —JAMES 4:6, 10 (NIV)

PRAYER FOCUS

Father, You are the One who exalts Your children. I ask that You would lift up
_____ as he humbles himself before You. Give him eyes to see the
destructiveness of pride, and may _____ learn that humbly yielding
to Your lordship allows him to receive your power.

PERSONAL PRAYER

Because God knows your child and can search his heart, ask Him to reveal issues
you can't see. In light of what God knows, request that He use you to shape your
child's heart in attitudes of true humility.

Humility puts our children in a position to
receive the refreshing grace of God.

humility DAY FOUR

*I [Paul], by the grace God gave me, give this advice to each
one of you. Don't cherish exaggerated ideas of yourself or your
importance, but try to have a sane estimate of your capabilities.*
—ROMANS 12:3 (Phillips)

PRAYER FOCUS

Lord Jesus, You are the perfect God. I earnestly ask that _____ would
not have an attitude of superiority or perfectionism. Please allow _____
to see herself as one of Your wonderfully gifted creations. Grant her clear and
correct insight into the capabilities You have given her.

*Work happily together. Don't try to act big. Don't try to get into the good graces of
important people, but enjoy the company of ordinary folks. And don't think you know
it all!* —ROMANS 12:16 (TLB)

PRAYER FOCUS

Father, thank you that you free us to enjoy people of every status. I ask that you
give _____ the gift of humility. Supply _____ with a cor-
rect evaluation of herself regarding those with whom she will work and play. May
she not have a superior, arrogant, or know-it-all attitude.

PERSONAL PRAYER

Pray that your child's specific gifts would be used to their fullest to bless others—
filled with humility while willingly submitted to God's control.

*Humility is having a correct
evaluation of ourselves.*

humility DAY FIVE

We are not bold to class or compare ourselves with some
of those who commend themselves; but when they measure
themselves by themselves and compare themselves
with themselves, they are without understanding.

—2 CORINTHIANS 10:12 (NASB)

PRAYER FOCUS

Father, though You are exalted, You regard the lowly. I humbly pray that
_____ would be one of those who correctly evaluates himself. Keep
_____ from falling into the trap of comparing himself with others.

If any person thinks himself to be somebody [too important to condescend to shoulder
another's load] when he is nobody [of superiority except in his own estimation], he
deceives and deludes and cheats himself. —GALATIANS 6:3 (AMP)

PRAYER FOCUS

Lord God, I ask that You might take away from _____ any arrogant
attitude of superiority. I pray that _____ would not believe the lie, "I
have to be 'somebody' to be important." Entrust _____ with a spirit
of humility that is willing to meet another's need.

Pride leads to an incorrect estimation
of oneself in relation to others;
humility fosters a correct view of oneself.

you *and* me time

1. On separate index cards write down adjectives that describe family members and adjectives that don't (avoid words that are inflammatory), then spread the cards out on the floor. Let each child take turns selecting adjectives that describe him or her and passing over the ones that don't. Discuss how humility involves seeing ourselves the way God sees us: with accuracy and honesty; no greater and no less. Talk about how to respond when people compliment the talents God's given us, including the difference between a God-honoring response and a response of false humility.
2. Share with your child this interesting natural phenomenon: When two mountain goats meet on a steep and narrow mountain ledge, one of them will lie down and allow the other to pass over on top of him. Talk about the ways that humility at times requires that we "lie down" before others in the everyday confrontations of life.

live *it* out

1. When your child achieves a milestone, praise him or her fully—and attach that praise to God as well: "Great job on the test! I'm so proud of you! God has given you a lot of perseverance and intelligence, and it's so cool to see you honor Him with it."

humility

OBSERVATIONS, PRAYERS, AND ANSWERS

teachability

WILLINGNESS *to* LEARN *and* GROW

I have been driven many times to my knees by the overwhelming conviction that I had nowhere else to go.

—ABRAHAM LINCOLN

teachability DAY ONE

Teach me to do your will, for you are my God;
may your good Spirit lead me on level ground.
—Psalm 143:10 (NIV)

PRAYER FOCUS

Almighty God, I am so thankful that I can bring _____ to You in prayer. Look lovingly upon her, and teach her to do Your will because You are her God. Allow Your Spirit to lead her on level ground. Lord, guide _____ in her path today, that it would be the direction You would choose for her.

Guide me in your truth and teach me, for you are God my Savior, and my hope is in you all day long. —Psalm 25:5 (NIV)

PRAYER FOCUS

God and Savior, You alone are able to guide my child in the right path. I place _____ in Your loving care. I ask that You would instruct her in Your truth and teach her Your way. May _____'s hope be in You each and every day of her life.

Teachability is developing a heart attitude
that seeks God's guidance for living
to honor Him each day.

teachability DAY TWO

Then they would put their trust in God and would not forget his deeds but would keep his commands. They would not be like their forefathers—a stubborn and rebellious generation, whose hearts were not loyal to God, whose spirits were not faithful to him.

—PSALM 78:7–8 (NIV)

PRAYER FOCUS

Father, it is Your own Spirit who teaches us through Your Word. I pray that _____ would yield to Your instruction. Please protect him from developing a stubborn or rebellious spirit. May he be a spiritual sponge, soaking up Your truth.

Daniel resolved not to defile himself with the royal food and wine, and he asked the chief official for permission not to defile himself this way. —DANIEL 1:8 (NIV)

PRAYER FOCUS

Lord, You alone know the circumstances my child will face on any given day. I lift _____ before You and pray that he will prepare his heart to be faithful to You alone—no matter what circumstances he finds himself in. Father, begin to develop in _____ the courage and conviction to be a Daniel in his generation.

PERSONAL PRAYER

As you consider the various "voices" attempting to influence your child, ask God to protect him from those that would deter him from willingly following the voice of the Good Shepherd (John 10:5). Pray that teachers, friends, and counselors in your child's life would direct him closer to God.

Teachability helps our children prepare their hearts to be faithful to God.

teachability

The mind of the prudent is ever getting knowledge, and the ear
of the wise is ever seeking (inquiring for and craving) knowledge.
—Proverbs 18:15 (AMP)

PRAYER FOCUS

Father, I ask You to give _____ a teachable heart and an attentive attitude. Open her mind to the truth of Your Word, and make her ears sensitive to the godly wisdom of others.

Like an earring of gold or an ornament of fine gold is a wise man's rebuke to a listening ear. —Proverbs 25:12 (NIV)

PRAYER FOCUS

Lord, you are the Great Teacher. I pray that my child might have a wise and listening ear. Train _____ to be open to loving rebuke.

PERSONAL PRAYER

Ask God to nurture your child's teachability in areas where she is in need of reproof and/or discipline. Request His wisdom in applying the most appropriate methods and timing to address character issues in her life—and pray that He will prepare her heart by demonstrating her need for change in these areas.

Teachability is having a mind that seeks truth
and ears that are sensitive and willing
to hear knowledge and rebuke.

teachability DAY FOUR

*Every young man who listens to me and obeys my instructions will
be given wisdom and good sense. . . . For wisdom and truth will
enter the very center of your being, filling your life with joy.*

—Proverbs 2:1, 10 (TLB)

PRAYER FOCUS

Father, You are the giver of every good and perfect gift. Thank You that You want
to give wisdom and instruction to my child. Lord, I desire that the very center of
_____ 's being would be like a dry sponge soaking up Your sweet and
refreshing teachings.

*Thus says the LORD, "Let not a wise man boast of his wisdom, and let not the mighty
man boast of his might, let not a rich man boast of his riches; but let him who boasts
boast of this, that he understands and knows Me."* —Jeremiah 9:23-24 (NASB)

PRAYER FOCUS

God, you are the deep spring of all wisdom and knowledge that flows to us daily.
I humbly ask that _____ would not boast in his own wisdom but
would allow himself to be instructed in life by You, the giver of life. Grant him a
teachable spirit.

*Teachability is allowing ourselves
to be instructed by the Lord.*

teachability DAY FIVE

God disciplines us for our good, that we may share in his holiness.
No discipline seems pleasant at the time, but painful.
Later on, however, it produces a harvest of righteousness
and peace for those who have been trained by it.
—HEBREWS 12:10–11 (NIV)

PRAYER FOCUS

God of truth, deliver _____ from stubbornness. As she passes through each stage of life, may she learn to yield to those circumstances of life that You use to guide her into righteousness.

The man who is often reproved but refuses to accept criticism will suddenly be broken and never have another chance. —PROVERBS 29:1 (TLB)

PRAYER FOCUS

Father, it is my request that _____ be a child who is quick to accept criticism and to learn and grow from it. My prayer is that _____ would never have to be broken by You because of her stubbornness.

PERSONAL PRAYER

With faith in God's knowledge of—and power over—your child's heart, present to Him specific areas that indicate stubbornness, pride, and/or an inability to accept criticism.

A stubborn heart changes only under the
pressure of negative circumstances;
a teachable heart responds willingly to correction.

you *and* me time

1. To stimulate mealtime conversation, discuss the following questions:
   - What are the characteristics of a teachable person?
   - Why it is difficult to listen to and accept criticism?
2. Ask your children their opinion of who's the most teachable person . . .
   - in the Bible
   - in your family
   - they've ever known

live *it* out

1. Create a climate of teachability by "racing" your children or spouse to the cross: Be the first to genuinely repent, seeking forgiveness and restoration when you've wronged them. Don't let repentance be unusual in your home, whether by parents *or* children. Express your compassionate, heartfelt "I'm sorry for . . . [specific action]. I was wrong to be . . . [heart attitude]. That must have made you feel . . . [emotion]. Would you forgive me?" After times of conflict with your child or spouse, take time to pray together for forgiveness and God's change in your hearts, thanking Him for Jesus' sacrifice, which allows both of you to be forgiven.
2. Ask your children questions about your own character. Without attempting to defend yourself, demonstrate teachability by listening and gently, humbly responding. You might start with, "What are some things you like about the way I parent you?" And then, "How do you think I could be more like God in the way I act?" Your children will be more likely to approach you later, too, because of your appreciative response to their honesty. Without granting your children undue authority over your life, ask the Holy Spirit to use them to demonstrate ways God would like to change you—and help you love your children even better.

teachability

OBSERVATIONS, PRAYERS, AND ANSWERS

forgiveness

YIELDING *the* RIGHT *to* INJURE *an* OFFENDER *in* RETURN

In the very truest sense, intercession is love on its knees.

—DICK EASTMAN

forgiveness DAY ONE

In him [Jesus] we have redemption through his blood,
the forgiveness of sins, in accordance
with the riches of God's grace.

—EPHESIANS 1:7 (NIV)

PRAYER FOCUS

Gracious Father, we thank You that _____ has been/can be set free
by the blood of Christ through His death on the cross. May _____
understand that he has forgiveness of sins because of Your grace.

Where is another God like you, who pardons the sins of the survivors among his people?
You cannot stay angry with your people, for you love to be merciful. Once again you
will have compassion on us. You will tread our sins beneath your feet; you will throw
them into the depths of the ocean! —MICAH 7:18–19 (TLB)

PRAYER FOCUS

Father, I thank You for being such a merciful God. Help _____ not to be
hesitant in coming to You in confession and repentance. Touch _____'s
heart with an understanding of how completely You forgive when he repents of
his sin and returns to You.

PERSONAL PRAYER

If you suspect that your child may have an unrepentant spirit regarding certain
sins in his life, ask God to soften his heart and overwhelm him with mercy and a
willingness to forgive. Pray that your child would regularly bask in God's mercy,
keenly aware of his need for a Savior.

Forgiveness is God's gift to us through the death
and resurrection of Jesus Christ. It allows us to
have new life and eternal fellowship with God.

forgiveness DAY TWO

"Do not judge, and you will not be judged; and do
not condemn, and you will not be condemned;
pardon, and you will be pardoned."
—LUKE 6:37 (NASB)

PRAYER FOCUS

Father, give _____ a forgiving spirit. Help her not to condemn the
weaknesses of others. Give _____ the strength to give up any resentment she is harboring, which can grow out of a failure to forgive others.

Even if [your brother] sins against you seven times in a day, and turns to you seven
times and says, I repent [I am sorry], you must forgive him (give up resentment and
consider the offense as recalled and annulled). —LUKE 17:4 (AMP)

PRAYER FOCUS

Father, help _____ endure in forgiveness and repeatedly forgive
those who fail her and You. Guard _____ from becoming critical and
judgmental when she is faced with the weaknesses and failures of others.

Forgiveness frees us from a judgmental
and critical spirit.

forgiveness DAY THREE

*Never pay back evil for evil. Do things in such a way that
everyone can see you are honest clear through. Don't quarrel with
anyone. Be at peace with everyone, just as much as possible. Dear
friends, never avenge yourselves. Leave that to God, for he has
said that he will repay those who deserve it.*
—ROMANS 12:17–19 (TLB)

PRAYER FOCUS

Dear God, I pray that _____ would be willing to learn not to repay
evil for evil. Help him to learn what true love is—the love that Christ has for us.
Teach _____ that he must not try to get even, but leave that up to
You. Lord, help _____ see that forgiveness can break the cycle of
retribution and bring healing to relationships. And may _____ discover how right actions can lead to right attitudes.

*When [people] hurled their insults at [Jesus], he did not retaliate; when he suf-
fered, he made no threats. Instead, he entrusted himself to him who judges justly.*
—1 PETER 2:23 (NIV)

PRAYER FOCUS

Dear God, thank you for sending your Son to be the ultimate example of forgiveness. May _____ be willing to love others and forgive them in spite
of their wrong attitudes and behavior. Help him see that responding wisely and
gently in a tough situation can soften hearts.

PERSONAL PRAYER

Ask God to be Lord over your child's anger—that it would be a tool for righteousness rather than evil. Pray that God would teach him to be self-controlled, to manage his tongue, and to be slow to anger. Ask God to bring positive influences into
your child's life to teach reconciliation and wise anger management.

*Forgiveness is responding to evil
by doing good.*

forgiveness DAY FOUR

"Forgive our sins—for we have forgiven those
who sinned against us."
—LUKE 11:4 (TLB)

PRAYER FOCUS

Dear Father, speak to _____'s heart about forgiveness. Help her see
the need to receive your forgiveness for her sin. May _____ then see
the need to forgive those who have wronged or offended her.

"When you are praying, first forgive anyone you are holding a grudge against, so that
your Father in heaven will forgive you your sins too." —MARK 11:25 (TLB)

PRAYER FOCUS

Lord, I know Your desire is to forgive _____ when she is separated
from You by sin in her life. I truly pray that she would not be a person who holds
grudges but would quickly and joyfully forgive others.

PERSONAL PRAYER

Talk to God about areas in your child's life in which she may find it difficult to
forgive. Ask that she would understand the extent to which she's been forgiven,
and that she would experience the freedom and blessedness of offering forgiveness in those situations—absorbing the guilt of another, as Jesus did for us, and
demonstrating His love and character (read Psalm 103).

Forgiveness is the gift we must receive
in order to forgive others.

forgiveness DAY FIVE

Do not repay evil with evil or insult with insult, but with blessing,
because to this you were called so that you may inherit a blessing.
—1 PETER 3:9 (NIV)

PRAYER FOCUS

Almighty God, You alone have the right to repay the evil that others have done
to us. May _____ accept your promise of justice and choose not to
show revenge for the wrong others have done to him. In turn, help _____
to give a blessing instead, that others will know that he belongs to You.

Above all, love each other deeply, because love covers over a multitude of sins.
—1 PETER 4:8 (NIV)

PRAYER FOCUS

Father, I pray that _____ would come to recognize the deep need to
not retaliate in revenge but to forgive those who offend him. Release him from
any attitude of revenge in his life. May _____'s eyes be fixed on Jesus
Christ and not on the insults of others. Lord, bring to _____'s mind
his own weaknesses so that he might have compassion for the weaknesses of others. Help him to see that love covers a multitude of sins.

Revenge is the act of inflicting punishment or injury in
return for what one has suffered at the hand of another;
forgiveness releases a person from the offense
and leaves judgment in God's hands.

you *and* me time

1. Have someone read aloud Matthew 7:3. Bring a fireplace-sized log and place it in different spots around the house throughout the week to remind everyone daily to forgive others and get the "log" out of their own eyes before trying to critically get the speck out of someone else's eye.
2. If you have older children, watch the movie *Les Misérables* (1998) together. Discuss the power of forgiveness and grace (undeserved favor) in the life of Jean Valjean—and contrast this with the traits of Inspector Javert.

live *it* out

1. If you have a child who's struggling to forgive, take him or her on an individual outing, full of time to explore what's going on in your child's life, and have some fun together. Later in the evening, in a private setting (like a walk outdoors), honestly relate to your child a situation from your own life in which you felt great anger and struggled to forgive, but God eventually gave you victory. (Tip: if your child knows the individual who hurt you, consider protecting that person's identity to keep your child from additional anger or bitterness toward him or her.) Discuss your continued choice to lay aside your anger, as God did for you both by sending His own Son to die on the cross. Then gently and compassionately express your concern over your child's struggle to forgive, and pray with him or her. Don't forget to pray in advance that God will give your child a soft, teachable heart.

forgiveness

OBSERVATIONS, PRAYERS, AND ANSWERS

obedience

COMPLYING, FROM *the* HEART, *with* GOD'S DESIRES *for* US

Prayer lifts the heart above the battles of life and gives it a glimpse of God's resources which spell victory and hope.

—C. NEIL STRAIT

obedience DAY ONE

Children, obey your parents in the Lord [as His representatives],
for this is just and right. Honor (esteem and value as precious)
your father and your mother.
—Ephesians 6:1–2 (amp)

PRAYER FOCUS

Lord, I ask that _____ would eagerly and willingly obey us as her
parents. Allow her to recognize and joyfully accept the fact that we are Your
representatives to guide and direct her—and Father, please give us wisdom as
_____ 's parents. We want to be valued as precious in her eyes.

[Jesus] went down with [His parents] and came to Nazareth and was [habitually]
obedient to them . . . And Jesus increased in wisdom (in broad and full understanding)
and in stature and years, and in favor with God and man. —Luke 2:51–52 (amp)

PRAYER FOCUS

Dear God, I pray that _____ would become consistently obedient in
every area of her life. Cultivate in her the desire to develop godly habits through
obedience to the Word of God.

PERSONAL PRAYER

Lift to God specific areas in which your child currently and habitually resists
obedience.

Obedience puts children in proper
relation to their parents—God's
representative authorities.

obedience DAY TWO

Let every person be loyally subject to the governing (civil)
authorities. For there is no authority except
from God [by His permission].
—ROMANS 13:1 (AMP)

PRAYER FOCUS

Father, impart to _____ the willingness to be submissive to the many
governing and ruling authorities in our country. Develop in _____ a
deep respect for the laws of our land and for those who enforce them, a mind for
Your thoughts, and a desire to be active in the development of our country.

Remind people to be submissive to [their] magistrates and authorities, to be obedient, . . .
and to show unqualified courtesy toward everybody. —TITUS 3:1–2 (AMP)

PRAYER FOCUS

Father, may Your Holy Spirit remind _____ to be submissive to his
teachers in school and church, his coaches, and authorities in other establish-
ments. Convey to _____ the need to show them courtesy and respect
by being quick to do what he is told, within the constraints of God's law.

Obedience puts children in proper relation to
the outside authorities in their lives—teachers,
church leaders, police, and others.

obedience DAY THREE

"God sees not as man sees, for man looks at the outward appearance, but the LORD looks at the heart."

—1 SAMUEL 16:7 (NASB)

PRAYER FOCUS

Lord, I want to thank You and to trust You for a child who is obedient in her behavior. I pray that Your Holy Spirit might drive deeper into _____'s soul an attitude and spirit of obedience. Give _____ the understanding that You see the things she does in secret and that You even know her innermost thoughts.

What does the Lord your God require of you but [reverently] to fear the Lord your God, [that is] to walk in all His ways, and to love Him, and to serve the Lord your God with all your [mind and] heart and with your entire being. —DEUTERONOMY 10:12 (AMP)

PRAYER FOCUS

Father, instill in _____ a desire to obey You. I ask that she would obey me not because I'm the parent but because You have put within her a reverence for You and for Your Word.

Obedience is a heart attitude that should characterize the spirit of my child; it is not just an outward act.

obedience DAY FOUR

"No one can serve two masters. Either he will hate the one and love the other, or he will be devoted to the one and despise the other. You cannot serve both God and Money."
—MATTHEW 6:24 (NIV)

PRAYER FOCUS

Heavenly Father, I ask You to save _____ from the trap of spending his life desiring and pursuing material possessions. Fill his mind with Your thoughts instead of the voices of materialism. Allow _____ to find the inner beauty and strength that come from obeying You, not from gaining possessions.

"If anyone would come after me [Jesus], he must deny himself and take up his cross daily and follow me. . . . What good is it for a man to gain the whole world, and yet lose or forfeit his very self?" —LUKE 9:23, 25 (NIV)

PRAYER FOCUS

Lord, cause _____ to see that although many people choose not to obey You, he must make his own commitment to take up his cross and follow You. Give him the strength to uphold his commitment to You even when it gets tough. Father, may _____'s resolve to obey You be a shield and protection from the forces that desire to press him into the world's mold.

Obedience puts material things into proper perspective and shields our children from the dangers of peer pressure.

obedience DAY FIVE

"Don't be frightened," Samuel reassured [the people].
"You have certainly done wrong, but make sure now that
you worship the Lord with true enthusiasm, and that you
don't turn your back on him in any way."
—1 SAMUEL 12:20 (TLB)

PRAYER FOCUS

Lord, thank You for Your mercy even when we disobey. I ask that _____
would see clearly when she is wrong and disobedient to You and would be quick
to seek Your forgiveness. Show her how to worship You with true enthusiasm and
not turn her back on You in any way.

[Delilah] nagged at [Samson] every day until he couldn't stand it any longer and
finally told her his secret. "My hair has never been cut," he confessed, "for I've been a
Nazirite to God since before my birth. If my hair were cut, my strength would leave me,
and I would become as weak as anyone else." —JUDGES 16:16–17 (TLB)

PRAYER FOCUS

Father, please grant _____ the strength to withstand the temptation
to willfully disobey You and Your Word—no matter how insistent others may be
in trying to persuade her to compromise or disobey. Lord, support her so she
remains firm in her obedience to You.

Disobedience is willfully choosing not to
follow a command or law; obedience chooses to
submit to authority even when it's difficult.

you *and* me time

1. Help your young child make a mobile that reflects God's chain of command for the home. Be sure to put God at the top, followed by Dad, Mom, and then the kids.
2. Have your child write out a list of authorities in his or her life. Post the list where it's easy to see (or have an older child tuck the list in his or her Bible), and encourage your child to pray for a different authority each day.
3. Make popsicles or Jell-O together using different molds. Talk about how God's Word molds and shapes our lives too.

live *it* out

1. First Timothy 5:17 tells us that "the elders who direct the affairs of the church well are worthy of double honor, especially those whose work is preaching and teaching" (NIV). Develop a plan to honor the pastor(s) of your church, caring for him and showing your appreciation by sending him a letter or card, packing him a gift basket, preparing a favorite dessert, or inviting him to dinner.
2. When you see police officers, coaches, teachers, and other authority figures, thank them for their service. Children can make cards, letters, cookies, or small gifts for those in authority who regularly invest in their lives.
3. Develop a reward chart to keep track of occasions when a child obeys "without complaining or arguing" (Philippians 2:14, NIV). You might list his or her regular responsibilities, keeping track of your child's completion of each task with stickers—and culminating in another small reward.

obedience

OBSERVATIONS, PRAYERS, AND ANSWERS

discernment

WISE JUDGMENT FULL *of* KEEN INSIGHT

Prayer is not conquering God's reluctance, but taking hold of God's willingness.

—PHILLIPS BROOKS

discernment DAY ONE

My son, if you accept my words and store up my commands within
you, turning your ear to wisdom and applying your heart to
understanding, and if you call out for insight and cry aloud for
understanding, and if you look for it as for silver and search for it
as for hidden treasure, then you will understand the fear of the
Lord and find the knowledge of God. For the Lord gives wisdom,
and from his mouth come knowledge and understanding.
—Proverbs 2:1–6 (niv)

PRAYER FOCUS

God, help _____ listen to wisdom and seek with all his heart to gain understanding. Cause him to listen to what I say and remember what I have asked of him. Lord, lead _____ in earnestly seeking wisdom and understanding. Open his eyes to search for it just as he would for silver or for hidden treasure. Then _____ will understand what it means to respect You, Lord, for only You give wisdom and knowledge and understanding.

"Solid food" is only for the adult, that is, for the man who has developed by experience his power to discriminate between what is good and what is evil. —Hebrews 5:14 (Phillips)

PRAYER FOCUS

Dear God, develop discernment in _____ because he has practiced doing what is right again and again. Permit _____ to see and experience the inner victory and confidence that come from wise discernment.

Discernment is a reward for persistently
searching for wisdom and insight.

discernment DAY TWO

Conduct yourselves with wisdom toward outsiders, making the
most of the opportunity. Let your speech always be with grace,
as though seasoned with salt, so that you will know
how you should respond to each person.

—COLOSSIANS 4:5–6 (NASB)

PRAYER FOCUS

God, please entrust to _____ wisdom in the way she acts toward
people, especially unbelievers. Reveal to her how to use her time wisely. When
she speaks, season her words with kindness and wisdom so she can answer everyone in the way she should.

Do not be quick with your mouth, do not be hasty in your heart to utter anything
before God. God is in heaven and you are on earth, so let your words be few.
—ECCLESIASTES 5:2 (NIV)

PRAYER FOCUS

Dear Lord, guide _____ in how she speaks. Liberate her from being
quick to speak and hasty in her heart to say things before You. Cause her to see
the wisdom of using discretion in her speech and making her words count for
good—even if it means saying less!

PERSONAL PRAYER

Scripture puts great emphasis on the power of the tongue. Pray that God will
help your child overcome specific weaknesses in the way she uses her words, and
praise God for the character you've seen your child exhibit in that area as well,
asking God to use those strengths for His honor.

Discernment is using wise judgment
in our speech and thoughts.

discernment DAY THREE

Wisdom and good judgment live together, for wisdom knows where to discover knowledge and understanding. If anyone respects and fears God, he will hate evil. For wisdom hates pride, arrogance, corruption and deceit of every kind.

—PROVERBS 8:12–13 (TLB)

PRAYER FOCUS

Loving Father, teach _____ ways he can demonstrate that "wisdom and good judgment live together" in his life. Please help him to know where to discover knowledge and understanding. Lord, I ask that _____ would always respect and fear You and hate what is evil. Help him learn to hate the sins of pride, arrogance, and corruption.

The prudent sees the evil and hides himself, but the naive go on, and are punished for it. —PROVERBS 22:3 (NASB)

PRAYER FOCUS

Merciful God, stand by _____ in all he does so that he will become a wise, discerning person. Help him to sense when danger is ahead and be determined to avoid it. Keep him, Lord, from being foolish and walking into trouble.

PERSONAL PRAYER

Ask God for wisdom in specific areas in which your child needs guidance right now.

Discernment leads to making wise choices.

discernment

A wise man is cautious and turns away from evil,
but a fool is arrogant and careless.

—PROVERBS 14:16 (NASB)

PRAYER FOCUS

Merciful heavenly Father, I ask you to give _____ discernment and wisdom. In this world full of subtle evils, may she be sensitive and cautious about her decisions and directions in life.

Be self-controlled and alert. Your enemy the devil prowls around like a roaring lion looking for someone to devour. —1 PETER 5:8 (NIV)

PRAYER FOCUS

My God, you are the all-seeing One. Open _____'s eyes to see the evil that lurks around her. Protect her from the Enemy, who is looking for an opportunity to devour her. Lord, may _____ literally flee from evil and avoid the consequences of indiscretion by practicing self-control.

PERSONAL PRAYER

Request God's protection and discernment for your child in particular situations of concern.

Discernment is seeing, understanding,
and avoiding a potential evil and its consequences.

discernment DAY FIVE

The simpleton believes every word he hears, but the prudent man looks and considers well where he is going.

—PROVERBS 14:15 (AMP)

PRAYER FOCUS

Wise and discerning God, keep _____ from repeated indiscretion and foolishness. Cause him to learn quickly from his mistakes and not to foolishly repeat them. Give _____ discernment that keeps him from believing everything he hears.

As a dog returns to its vomit, so a fool repeats his folly. —PROVERBS 26:11 (NIV)

PRAYER FOCUS

Father, to repeat a mistake is not good, but to return to a folly is so very foolish. Teach _____ to see through the foolishness of the world's attitudes and actions. Keep him from returning to folly even if "friends" encourage him strongly to do so. Grant him relationships that encourage him in wise, God-fearing decisions.

PERSONAL PRAYER

Ask for God's insight for your child in the midst of specific lies he may be prone to believe.

Foolishness is the repeated gullibility and indiscretion of the naive; discernment honors God in each wise decision.

you *and* me time

1. To emphasize that discernment senses danger and keeps us from walking into trouble, play a blindfold game. Choose a family member to be blindfolded. Another family member can be the designated "voice of discernment" who will direct the blindfolded member around obstacles (cushions, pillows, chairs) toward a goal or reward—like a favorite snack in the kitchen. Other family members are the "distracting voices of the world," attempting to shout false directions to steer the blindfolded family member off course.
2. Play the "What If" game. Present your child with a moral dilemma and talk through what a wise solution would look like. Books like the *Sticky Situations* devotionals (Betsy Schmitt, Tyndale Kids, 2006) may help.

live *it* out

1. Allow your child—possibly with a sibling—to plan a family night, with a small budget for snacks or entertainment that he or she is responsible to use with wisdom and discernment. As your children progress in age, place other small budgets in their care as they're able. Work with them to use a budget for wisely purchasing all their clothing, or set up an entertainment budget that allows them some social interaction but requires that they make choices.
2. When possible, invite your child's friends to your home or on outings with your family. Get to know your child's friends as well as some of the temptations your child may be facing, and use the opportunity to expose those friends to the "light" of Jesus Christ in your family, especially in the way you love one another. Let your child know that when faced with temptation or invited to an event he or she shouldn't attend, you don't mind being an "out": "My parents said no" or "No way would my folks let me do that!"

discernment

OBSERVATIONS, PRAYERS, AND ANSWERS

purity

Of a SINGLE SUBSTANCE; FREE *of* THAT WHICH SPOILS

God's pray-ers are societies' best revolutionaries.

—DICK EASTMAN

purity DAY ONE

*Run from anything that gives you the evil thoughts that young
men often have, but stay close to anything that makes you
want to do right. . . . Enjoy the companionship of those
who love the Lord and have pure hearts.*
—2 TIMOTHY 2:22 (TLB)

PRAYER FOCUS

Father, provide _____ the wisdom and strength to flee from anything
that would stir up inappropriate desires. Give her a godly desire to have a pure
mind and to seek friendships with those who have pure hearts.

*I will set before my eyes no vile thing. The deeds of faithless men I hate; they will not
cling to me. Men of perverse heart shall be far from me; I will have nothing to do with
evil.* —PSALM 101:3–4 (NIV)

PRAYER FOCUS

Holy God, I ask that _____ would have a commitment to only look
at pure things and to have pure thoughts. Teach her that fantasies arouse feelings that can easily lead to sinful actions. Help her to understand that evil companions stir up evil desires.

PERSONAL PRAYER

Ask God to guard your child against specific traps that threaten her purity of
mind, heart, and body.

*Purity is avoiding activities and companions
that stir up evil thoughts.*

purity DAY TWO

God wants you to be holy and pure, and to keep clear of all sexual
sin so that each of you will marry in holiness and honor.
—1 THESSALONIANS 4:3–4 (TLB)

PRAYER FOCUS

Father, I ask that you give _____ a commitment to purity in his
sexual life. Put a hedge around him and protect him from the temptations and
persuasiveness of his own flesh and our culture.

Do not let sin control your puny body any longer; do not give in to its sinful desires.
Do not let any part of your bodies become tools of wickedness, to be used for sinning.
—ROMANS 6:12–13 (TLB)

PRAYER FOCUS

Lord God, You are the Creator of both passion and purity. I pray that You would
give _____ self-control over his passions. May his desires not be
unbridled. I ask that he would not use any part of his body for impure purposes.

PERSONAL PRAYER

Pray for present and future influences that have the power to shape your child's
views of sexuality. Request God's protection for your child and his eyes. Ask
God to instill in your child self-restraint, wisdom in affections and choice of
companionship, and responsiveness to the Holy Spirit. Pray for your child's
future spouse, too, or your child's honor and purity in singleness, according to
God's will.

Purity is yielding to God by withholding our bodies
from unbiblical sexual involvement.

purity DAY THREE

Create in me a pure heart, O God,
and renew a steadfast spirit within me.

—PSALM 51:10 (NIV)

PRAYER FOCUS

Dear God and Father, I ask that _____ would continually come to
You recognizing her need to have a pure heart before You. Take away any wavering in her heart and renew a steadfast spirit within her so that she can follow You
wholeheartedly.

What I am eager for is that all the Christians there will be filled with love that
comes from pure hearts, and that their minds will be clean and their faith strong.
—1 TIMOTHY 1:5 (TLB)

PRAYER FOCUS

Lord, I pray that _____ will be filled with the kind of love that comes
from a pure heart, and that her mind will be clean and her faith will be strong.

Purity of heart is a gift from God.

you *and* me time

1. Place stalks of celery (complete with leaves) in a glass of water with food coloring (other than green) for a few days, and note how the celery takes on the water's color. Look up 1 Corinthians 15:33 and Philippians 4:8 together and talk about how the situations, people, and thoughts we choose "color" us.
2. Using 1 Corinthians 6:18, explain how the sexually impure person sins against or "bruises" his or her own body. Then take an unripe banana and repeatedly hit it, still in the peel, on a hard surface. In a few days, peel the banana and note the rotting that has taken place inside. What we do on the outside affects us on the inside.

live *it* out

1. Look for opportunities to reinforce that it is acceptable, even appropriate, to run from temptation. (With older children, you might read Joseph's response to temptation in Genesis 39.) Check out 1 Corinthians 10:12–13 together. Consider purity-threatening situations your child may face in the future (locker rooms, dates, slumber parties, an uncomfortable encounter with an adult, etc.) and discuss these scenarios, working together to find solutions that would provide a way out.
2. Instill principles that honor the purity of others. Boys can learn the foundational principle of manners by treating girls with respect, and girls can learn to graciously receive that respect. And both can learn to dress and carry their bodies in ways that don't encourage impure thoughts.
3. Consider the power of influence from your child's friends. Moms might take their daughters shopping for modest clothing with other moms and daughters with the same convictions or have a "spa night" that focuses on outer *and* inner beauty. Fathers may explore resources like the *Raising a Modern-Day Knight Training Pack* for a group of fathers to work through with their sons. They can also go to wholesome movies together or take a camping trip.

purity

OBSERVATIONS, PRAYERS, AND ANSWERS

responsibility

TRUSTWORTHINESS *to*
FULFILL OBLIGATIONS;
ACCOUNTABILITY *for*
CONDUCT

Prayer is a strong wall and fortress . . .
It is a goodly Christian weapon.

—MARTIN LUTHER

responsibility DAY ONE

*"I [Jesus] am the Good Shepherd. The Good Shepherd lays
down his life for the sheep . . . I am the Good Shepherd
and know my own sheep, and they know me."*
—JOHN 10:11, 14 (TLB)

PRAYER FOCUS

Father, I want _____ to learn from the example of the Lord Jesus—to
be willing to put aside his own feelings to meet the needs of others. Show him
that part of being responsible is learning to put others' needs above his own.

*Even if we believe that it makes no difference to the Lord whether we do these things
[eating meat offered to idols, drinking wine, or anything else that might cause someone
to stumble], still we cannot just go ahead and do them to please ourselves; for we must
bear the "burden" of being considerate of the doubts and fears of others—of those who
feel these things are wrong. Let's please the other fellow, not ourselves, and do what is
for his good and thus build him up in the Lord.* —ROMANS 15:1–2 (TLB)

PRAYER FOCUS

Dear God, I know there will be times when it will be hard for _____
to think of others instead of himself. Please give him a willingness to be considerate of the needs of others and to joyfully refrain from doing anything that might
cause someone else to stumble. Lord, I pray that _____ would
become sensitive and would desire to build others up in the Lord—and as a
result, be truly responsible.

*Responsibility is putting aside personal feelings
to help meet the needs of another.*

responsibility DAY TWO

I [Judah] will guarantee [Benjamin's] safety; you can
hold me personally responsible for him. If I do not bring
him back to you and set him here before you,
I will bear the blame before you all my life.

—GENESIS 43:9 (NIV)

PRAYER FOCUS

Dear God, help _____ understand the importance of taking responsibility in her life. Help her recognize, as Judah did, the opportunities before her
and then commit herself to a job with the determination to carry it out. Provide
_____ with the discipline and confidence needed to see the task
through to completion.

Now then [Joseph], please let your servant [Judah] remain here as my lord's slave in
place of the boy [Benjamin], and let the boy return with his brothers. How can I go
back to my father if the boy is not with me? No! Do not let me see the misery that would
come upon my father. —GENESIS 44:33–34 (NIV)

PRAYER FOCUS

Lord, instill in _____'s heart an understanding of what it means to
fulfill her obligations. When she is asked to take on new responsibilities, give her
discernment in her choices. Grant _____ the wisdom to realize that
in carrying out her responsibilities, her actions—good or bad—will affect other
people.

Responsibility is the determination
to fulfill one's obligations.

responsibility

*If you are unwilling to obey the Lord, then decide today whom you
will obey. . . . But as for me and my family, we will serve the Lord.*
—JOSHUA 24:15 (TLB)

PRAYER FOCUS

Lord, You are the one true God! My prayer for _____ is that he
would willingly choose to be faithful to You. May _____ be responsible in his choices and always commit himself to serve You.

*It was by faith that Moses, when he grew up, refused to be treated as the grandson of
the king, but chose to share ill-treatment with God's people instead of enjoying the fleet-
ing pleasures of sin.* —HEBREWS 11:24–25 (TLB)

PRAYER FOCUS

Father, like Moses, may my own child, _____, be willing to be ill-
treated rather than to live irresponsibly and choose wrongly. Lord, I ask that he
would be responsible and proud to be one of Your children, and avoid flirting
with sin.

PERSONAL PRAYER

Pray for your child as he confronts the specific temptations that oppose him as
he seeks to fulfill his responsibilities, and for the attitudes in his heart that make
such temptations a threat. Ask for God's wisdom in ways to expand your child's
sense of responsibility.

*Responsibility is choosing for oneself
between right and wrong.*

responsibility DAY FOUR

*As each one has received a special gift, employ it in serving one
another as good stewards of the manifold grace of God.*
—1 Peter 4:10 (NASB)

PRAYER FOCUS

Father, You are the giver of every good and perfect gift. Give me eyes to see how
You have gifted my child, and give _____ the sense of responsibility
to use her gifts to glorify You and serve others.

*We are God's workmanship, created in Christ Jesus to do good works, which God
prepared in advance for us to do.* —Ephesians 2:10 (NIV)

PRAYER FOCUS

Lord, You are the generous giver. I pray that _____ would follow
Your example. Fill her with a joyful spirit in carrying out the responsibilities for
which she is called.

PERSONAL PRAYER

Request God's insight into the way He's created your child, and how to carefully
hone those gifts to maximize for His use. Thank God for her unique gifts, talents,
opportunities, and resources.

*Responsibility is the obligation to use
the gifts and abilities God has given us.*

responsibility

Everyone who hears these words of Mine
and does not act on them, will be like a foolish man
who built his house on the sand.
—MATTHEW 7:26 (NASB)

PRAYER FOCUS

Father, protect _____ from being only a hearer of Your Word. Help him to be a doer of the Word as well—a young man of action. Deliver _____ from being controlled by a spirit of laziness that leads to repeated acts of irresponsibility. Thank You for hearing my prayer.

That slave who knew his master's will and did not get ready or act in accord with his will, will receive many lashes. —LUKE 12:47 (NASB)

PRAYER FOCUS

Lord, keep _____ safe from an "I don't care" attitude. Lift him up to be responsible in preparing himself to respond to Your voice and act according to Your will. Guard _____ from the negative influence of others.

Irresponsibility is laziness that fails to meet
the reasonable expectations of God and others,
but responsibility honors both.

you *and* me time

1. Involve your children in actions that joyfully embrace their responsibility as their "brother's keeper" (Genesis 4:9, NIV), such as cleaning up a neighbor's home or lawn, or providing childcare for someone who's ill or has recently had a baby.

2. Read 1 Corinthians 12 and Ephesians 4:7–16 together. Initiate a conversation (or set up a special date) in which you and your child take time to talk about the combination of personality traits, experiences, passions, giftings, and resources that God has given your child—and what it looks like to make the most of those for God's kingdom, now and in the future. You might both complete personality assessments, spiritual-gifts inventories, or even basic career testing, so that you can raise your child in light of who God's made him or her to be. Your child can also learn by observing you as you seek to serve well in your role as part of the body of Christ.

live *it* out

1. Hang up a "Good Job!" responsibility chart (using stickers and other small rewards) to help your child visibly track his or her completion of age-appropriate responsibilities.

2. Allow your child to handle increasing levels of responsibility in your home that mimic real-world responsibilities. Young children could be responsible for animal care and "teaching" younger siblings basic skills ("See? This is how I pick up my toys. We put the dolls in the basket . . ."). Elementary-school children could be in charge of making a dish for supper or planning a family night, and older children could manage a checking account, start a small business (like babysitting or lawn care), or cook a meal for the family.

responsibility
OBSERVATIONS, PRAYERS, AND ANSWERS

courage

PERSEVERING *with* CONFIDENCE *in* SPITE *of* DIFFICULTY, DANGER, PAIN, *or* FEAR

Prayer is not a little habit pinned on to us while we were tied to our mother's apron strings; neither is it a little decent quarter of a minute's grace said over an hour's dinner, but it is a most serious work of our most serious years.

—E. M. BOUNDS

courage DAY ONE

Shadrach, Meshach, and Abednego replied, "O Nebuchadnezzar,
we are not worried about what will happen to us.
If we are thrown into the flaming furnace, our God is able to
deliver us; and he will deliver us out of your hand, Your Majesty."
—DANIEL 3:16–17 (TLB)

PRAYER FOCUS

God, I pray that You will give _____ confidence that You are always
with her. Develop in her the assurance that she can courageously trust in You
and not worry about the future.

You know how badly we have been treated at Philippi just before we came to you, and
how much we suffered there. Yet God gave us the courage to boldly repeat the same mes-
sage to you, even though we were surrounded by enemies. —1 THESSALONIANS 2:2 (TLB)

PRAYER FOCUS

Father, I ask that You would give _____ the authentic courage to be
Your witness, even though some people will ridicule or reject her.

PERSONAL PRAYER

Your child knows much more intimately than you do the specific areas in which
she needs courage—and needs to sense God's trustworthy presence. Lift these
needs to God and pray that your child would continually be aware of God's faithfulness, growing to trust Him completely.

Courage is the strength of heart and mind
to confront an opponent with the confidence
that we will ultimately succeed.

courage DAY TWO

"Have I not commanded you? Be strong and courageous!
Do not tremble or be dismayed, for the LORD
your God is with you wherever you go."
—JOSHUA 1:9 (NASB)

PRAYER FOCUS

Mighty God who stands strong above every other power in heaven and earth, I pray that You would give _____ a tenacious courage. May he be able to face the dangers of his world—people, places, things—without panic and fear, but with strong confidence in You.

Even though I walk through the valley of the shadow of death, I will fear no evil, for you are with me; your rod and your staff, they comfort me. —PSALM 23:4 (NIV)

PRAYER FOCUS

Father, give _____ a radiant courage to face the dark places in his life. Focus his mind on the light and strength of Jesus Christ. Remove all panic from _____ that he may know You are always present and caring for him.

PERSONAL PRAYER

Pray that the Holy Spirit will fill your child with supernatural faith, peace, and joy in recurrent areas of fear in his life.

Courage is the strength of mind that helps
us to face danger without panic.

courage DAY THREE

"And now, compelled by the Spirit, I am going to Jerusalem, not knowing what will happen to me there. I only know that in every city the Holy Spirit warns me that prison and hardships are facing me. However, I consider my life worth nothing to me, if only I may finish the race and complete the task the Lord Jesus has given me—the task of testifying to the gospel of God's grace."

—ACTS 20:22–24 (NIV)

PRAYER FOCUS

Merciful Father, I lift _____ before You and pray that she would be willing to go wherever You lead. I pray that she would set her heart on following You at any cost. When she finds herself in a difficult place, give her courage and confidence in You alone. Lord, strengthen _____ to run the race and complete the task You have planned for her. I want her to be able to talk about the evidence of Your grace in her life.

"Be strong and courageous. Do not be afraid or terrified because of [the people you encounter], for the LORD your God goes with you; he will never leave you nor forsake you." —DEUTERONOMY 31:6 (NIV)

PRAYER FOCUS

Dear God, build up _____ to become a person who is strong and courageous because she trusts in You. As she faces people or circumstances that will test her convictions, help her not to be paralyzed by them but to always remember that You are with her.

PERSONAL PRAYER

Your child will face many obstacles in life that require great faith—and cannot be overcome apart from God's power. Pray that God would give her a faith that is equal to the task.

Courage is standing firm when facing adverse circumstances.

courage DAY FOUR

Now when Daniel learned that the decree [forbidding prayer to God] had been published, he went home to his upstairs room where the windows opened toward Jerusalem. Three times a day he got down on his knees and prayed, giving thanks to his God, just as he had done before. Then these men went as a group and found Daniel praying and asking God for help.

—DANIEL 6:10–11 (NIV)

PRAYER FOCUS

Lord God, my child will face many situations that will test his faith in You. Give him the courage to keep his eyes fixed on You. I pray that his commitment to You would become stronger than any other loyalty in his life. God, develop in _____ the character of Daniel—a loyal friend whose loyalty to You was unsurpassed.

PERSONAL PRAYER

Pray that loyalties that vie for the heart of your child might be removed, and that your child would repeatedly choose to show his loyalty to no other god but the true God.

Courage is putting confidence in God ahead of loyalty to others.

courage DAY FIVE

*Peter went over the side of the boat and walked on the water
toward Jesus. But when he looked around at the high waves, he
was terrified and began to sink. "Save me, Lord!" he shouted.
Instantly Jesus reached out his hand and rescued him.
"O man of little faith," Jesus said. "Why did you doubt me?"*
—MATTHEW 14:29–31 (TLB)

PRAYER FOCUS

Loving Father, give _____ grace when she finds herself overtaken by
fear. Lord, there are so many things in life that could cause her to live in fear.
Help keep her eyes on Jesus when she finds herself surrounded by the "high
waves" of life. I pray that she would learn to turn to your Son, Jesus, in her fear
and find that He is always sufficient.

*Soon a terrible storm arose. High waves began to break into the boat until it was nearly
full of water and about to sink. Jesus was asleep at the back of the boat with his head on
a cushion. Frantically they wakened him, shouting, "Teacher, don't you even care that
we are all about to drown?" Then he rebuked the wind and said to the sea, "Quiet
down!" And the wind fell, and there was a great calm! And he asked them, "Why were
you so fearful? Don't you even yet have confidence in me?"* —MARK 4:37–40 (TLB)

PRAYER FOCUS

Lord Jesus, when fear overtakes _____, help her to remember that
you can calm the fears of her heart just as you calmed the waves of the sea. In the
fearful things of _____'s life, show her the way to place herself in
Your sovereign control.

*When fear controls us and our faith is small,
the courageous call to Jesus, who is
always there to rescue us.*

you *and* me time

1. Read Daniel 6 together; then talk about what Daniel must have been feeling and why he made the decisions he did. You might ask your children to act out this chapter.
2. Find a local ropes course that families can participate in together (a guide is recommended). You'll have opportunities to push personal limits and enjoy a little adventure at the same time.
3. Read courage-inspiring stories together, such as those in *Growing Together in Courage* by Barbara Rainey (FamilyLife Publishing, 2010).

live *it* out

1. Hang a poster in your home titled "God Is Faithful in [year]!" As God demonstrates his consistent care for your family, record (as individuals and together) his special provisions throughout the year. Take time at least yearly (on New Year's Eve, perhaps) to thank God specifically for His kindnesses to your family and to express your trust in Him for the coming year.
2. As a family, pray about something God-sized—and ask what He would have you do about it.

courage

OBSERVATIONS, PRAYERS, AND ANSWERS

servanthood

LOVING THROUGH
LAYING DOWN *our*
INTERESTS *and* COMFORT
for ANOTHER

There is nothing that makes us love
man so much as praying for him.

—WILLIAM LAW

servanthood DAY ONE

We should be willing to be both vegetarians and teetotallers
or abstain from anything else if by doing otherwise we
should impede a brother's progress in the faith.
—ROMANS 14:21 (Phillips)

PRAYER FOCUS

Lord God, Your Son came as a servant of men. Instill within _____'s
heart a desire to become a servant to those around him. Help him be willing to
give up any freedom to help another person grow in faith.

Don't think only of yourself. Try to think of the other fellow, too, and what is best for
him. —1 CORINTHIANS 10:24 (TLB)

PRAYER FOCUS

Father, it is so hard to think of the other person first—or at all. Being a servant
sounds nice, but it takes effort. Give _____ a willingness to become
the kind of servant who doesn't mind putting out the effort and who looks out
for the good of the other person.

Servanthood is sacrificing one's own privileges
and liberties for the good of another.

servanthood DAY TWO

Do nothing out of selfish ambition or vain conceit, but in humility consider others better than yourselves. Each of you should look not only to your own interests, but also to the interests of others.

—PHILIPPIANS 2:3–4 (NIV)

PRAYER FOCUS

Lord God, I pray that You would work in _____'s life. I don't want selfishness or pride to control her. Teach her to be humble and to honor others more than herself. Lord, give _____ an interest in being involved in the lives of other people.

We who are strong ought to bear with the failings of the weak and not to please ourselves. Each of us should please his neighbor for his good, to build him up. For even Christ did not please himself. —ROMANS 15:1–3 (NIV)

PRAYER FOCUS

Father, open _____'s eyes to see the need to reach out to those around her with a servant's heart. Give _____ the willingness to always try to do what is good for others.

PERSONAL PRAYER

Speak with God about obstacles you see to your child's servanthood. Pray that she would seize opportunities to show His love within her various spheres of influence: school, church, and elsewhere.

Servanthood is a cure for selfishness.

servanthood DAY THREE

"The greatest among you will be your servant.
For whoever exalts himself will be humbled,
and whoever humbles himself will be exalted."
—MATTHEW 23:11–12 (NIV)

PRAYER FOCUS

Lord, help _____ take the first step toward seeing that in Your eyes,
the one who is willing to serve is greatest. God, work in _____'s life,
that he would learn to recognize the needs of others and allow You to use him in
meeting those needs.

"Anyone wanting to be a leader among you must be your servant. And if you want to
be right at the top, you must serve like a slave. Your attitude must be like my own, for
I, the Messiah, did not come to be served, but to serve, and to give my life as a ransom
for many." —MATTHEW 20:26–28 (TLB)

PRAYER FOCUS

Father, teach _____ the ways of leadership You desire: being a willing
servant and putting the needs of others above his own. Make this his heart's
desire and purpose, Lord. Develop in _____ the same attitude as
Your Son, Jesus, who came not to be served but to serve.

PERSONAL PRAYER

Each of us leads someone—and your child may one day lead his own family. Pray
that he will use the power or blessing he's been given for the purpose of blessing
others.

Servanthood keeps us aware of another's needs.

servanthood

[Jesus] got up from the meal . . . and began to wash the disciples' feet. . . .
When he had finished . . . he put on his clothes and returned to his place.
"Do you understand what I have done for you?" he asked them.
"You call me 'Teacher' and 'Lord,' and rightly so, for that is what
I am. Now that I, your Lord and Teacher, have washed your feet,
you also should wash one another's feet. I have set you an example
that you should do as I have done for you . . . Now that you know
these things, you will be blessed if you do them."
—JOHN 13:4–5, 12–15, 17 (NIV)

PRAYER FOCUS

Most loving God, I thank You that Your Son was willing to be a servant to man.
I thank You for the example He gave us of serving others. Help _____
to develop a heart for serving others as she learns of Christ's example. Lord, help
_____ choose to demonstrate a servant's heart.

Though I am free from all men, I have made myself a slave to all, that I may win more.
—1 CORINTHIANS 9:19 (NASB)

PRAYER FOCUS

Almighty God, I ask that You would lead _____ to be a servant of all
people, that she might draw them to You. I pray that she would willingly under-
take this humble service, and by doing so, that she would experience true spiritual greatness.

PERSONAL PRAYER

Pray that your child will enthusiastically serve those in her life right now in order
to show them Christ and his love for others.

Servanthood is spiritual greatness demonstrated
through humility and servitude.

servanthood DAY FIVE

"I was hungry, and you gave Me nothing to eat; I was thirsty,
and you gave Me nothing to drink; I was a stranger,
and you did not invite Me in; naked, and you did not clothe Me."
—MATTHEW 25:42–43 (NASB)

PRAYER FOCUS

Father, deliver _____ from this great weakness of the flesh—selfishness! Help him to become a servant to others. Help him to be sensitive to the physical and emotional needs of those around him.

Who is wise and understanding among you? Let him show it by his good life, by deeds done in the humility that comes from wisdom. But if you harbor bitter envy and selfish ambition in your hearts, do not boast about it or deny the truth. . . . For where you have envy and selfish ambition, there you find disorder and every evil practice.
—JAMES 3:13–14, 16 (NIV)

PRAYER FOCUS

Lord Jesus, keep _____ from seeking his own self-interest. Guard him from selfish ambition and from looking out for his own needs at the expense of others' needs. Show him ways he can demonstrate servanthood by having a generous and humble spirit characterized by good deeds.

Self-interest is providing for oneself at the
expense of others, while serving places
others' needs above one's own.

you *and* me time

1. Plan to have a "servanthood meal" for your family. Prepare the following place settings:
   - One plate: Large double portions of the entire meal, including a drink and dessert.
   - One (or more) plates: A small portion of everything—without dessert.
   - One (or more) plates: Bread and water.
   - One plate: Nothing.

   Arrange the plates on your countertop and allow family members to serve themselves, "first come, first served." Let the meal continue until those with an abundance see the need to share with others and take responsible actions to do so. By way of application, you can also draw a comparison between recognizing and meeting the needs within your family and the needs of all people worldwide.

2. Grab a towel and a basin of water, and then read John 13:1–17 together. After this, as parents, wash your children's feet, and then each other's feet, discussing the significance of this act.

live *it* out

1. Plan a family service project together. Pray about whom God would have you serve, asking Him to demonstrate the most effective ways in which to love that person or organization. (You might ask the person you're aiming to serve what he or she needs most, making sure the person doesn't feel you're being condescending.) Make a budget as a family and open it up to contributions from allowances, too. After your service project is complete, take photos and celebrate together with a small reward, such as going out for ice cream.

servanthood

OBSERVATIONS, PRAYERS, AND ANSWERS

contentment

CHOOSING, *in* FAITH, SATISFACTION *with* ONE'S SITUATION

One may lack talent for doing great things, as men count greatness, but one's station in life does not determine greatness in the sight of God. He looks for dedicated hearts carrying prayerful burdens. God longs for those who work at prayer.

—DICK EASTMAN

contentment DAY ONE

The LORD is good to those who wait for Him,
to the person who seeks Him. It is good that he waits
silently for the salvation of the LORD.
—LAMENTATIONS 3:25–26 (NASB)

PRAYER FOCUS

Father, give _____ the ability to see that You give your best to those
who wait on You. I ask, Lord, that _____ would possess a genuine
contentment with herself as a person, as well as in the circumstances she faces
each day.

I would have despaired unless I had believed that I would see the goodness of the LORD
in the land of the living. Wait for the LORD; be strong and let your heart take courage;
yes, wait for the LORD. —PSALM 27:13–14 (NASB)

PRAYER FOCUS

Lord, teach _____ to have the contentment that hopes in You. Give
her the assurance that leads to inner peace, tranquility, and contentment.
Strengthen _____'s faith in Your goodness when she is tempted to
despair.

Contentment is realizing that God can
provide an inner peace and tranquility
regardless of the situation.

contentment DAY TWO

*My heart is not proud, O LORD, my eyes are not haughty; I do not
concern myself with great matters or things too wonderful for
me. But I have stilled and quieted my soul; like a weaned child
with its mother, like a weaned child is my soul within me.*
—PSALM 131:1–2 (NIV)

PRAYER FOCUS

Merciful God, instill in my child a heart that is not proud and eyes that are not
haughty. Enable _____ to place the concerns of his life confidently
in Your care. I pray that my child would find favor in Your eyes. Lord, give him a
spirit that is still and quiet before You.

*Be delighted with the Lord. Then he will give you all your heart's desires. Commit every-
thing you do to the Lord. Trust him to help you do it and he will.* —PSALM 37:4–5 (TLB)

PRAYER FOCUS

Lord, You alone are our true contentment. Help _____ to understand that gaining genuine contentment comes as he learns to delight himself in
knowing You. Help _____ see that as he commits himself to You in
quiet trust, he will experience real contentment.

*Genuine contentment is established
in a quiet trust in the Lord.*

contentment DAY THREE

*Do not be anxious about anything, but in everything, by prayer
and petition, with thanksgiving, present your requests to God. And
the peace of God, which transcends all understanding, will guard
your hearts and minds in Christ Jesus. . . . My God will meet all
your needs according to his glorious riches in Christ Jesus.*
—Philippians 4:6–7, 19 (niv)

PRAYER FOCUS

Loving God, comfort _____ when she is hurting or filled with anxiety. Sustain her with Your grace and gently remind her that You will meet her
needs. As _____ learns to depend on You in this way, help her to
experience true contentment.

*God is able to make all grace abound to you, so that in all things at all times, having all
that you need, you will abound in every good work.* —2 Corinthians 9:8 (niv)

PRAYER FOCUS

Father, I thank You for the many ways You have blessed and provided for
_____. Confirm in her heart all that You have done for her. Show
her that You have given her even more than she's asked for. Allow her to see
ways that she can share her abundance with others.

PERSONAL PRAYER

Pray for contented faith in whatever circumstances are causing your child
anxiety.

*Contentment comes in understanding that
it is God who supplies our needs.*

contentment DAY FOUR

*Not that I was ever in need, for I have learned how to get along happily whether
I have much or little. I know how to live on almost nothing or with everything. I
have learned the secret of contentment in every situation, whether it be a full
stomach or hunger, plenty or want; for I can do everything God asks me to with
the help of Christ who gives me the strength and power.*
—PHILIPPIANS 4:11–13 (TLB)

PRAYER FOCUS

Dear Lord, our society doesn't understand the meaning of contentment very
well. It's going to be hard for _____ to battle the influences of greed
all around him. Show him that the way to true contentment in life comes not
from having all he wants but through joyful obedience to Your Son, Jesus. Help
him to understand that he can do everything You ask of him with Christ's help.

*[The Lord] said to me [Paul], "My grace is sufficient for you, for my power is made
perfect in weakness." Therefore I will boast all the more gladly about my weaknesses,
so that Christ's power may rest on me. That is why, for Christ's sake, I delight in weaknesses, in insults, in hardships, in persecutions, in difficulties. For when I am weak,
then I am strong.* —2 CORINTHIANS 12:9–10 (NIV)

PRAYER FOCUS

Father, You alone are sufficient for all of our needs. I ask that Your Spirit would
give _____ an understanding heart in this area. Help him to know
that You are sufficient for him, even in his greatest weaknesses and struggles.
Help _____ to see that he can be joyfully content wherever he is,
knowing that in You he is strong even when he is weak.

PERSONAL PRAYER

Think of some of your child's greatest joys. Pray that he would associate those
joys with their Giver—and not merely focus on the gifts.

*Contentment is the result of responding
to Christ in joyful obedience.*

contentment DAY FIVE

I envied the arrogant when I saw the prosperity of the wicked. . . .
When I tried to understand all this, it was oppressive to
me till I entered the sanctuary of God; then I understood
their final destiny. . . . Whom have I in heaven but you?
And earth has nothing I desire besides you.
—PSALM 73:3, 16–17, 25 (NIV)

PRAYER FOCUS

Father, give _____ victory over any spirit of covetousness. Keep
_____ from becoming greedy or envious of those whose goal in life is
to acquire status or possessions.

People who long to be rich soon begin to do all kinds of wrong things to get money,
things that hurt them and make them evil-minded and finally send them to hell itself.
—1 TIMOTHY 6:9 (TLB)

PRAYER FOCUS

Lord, You want to provide our every need. Help _____ find contentment in You alone. Take away from her any love of money. Show her how to
honor You with her money by using it wisely.

Covetousness leads to the greed and envy
of the unrighteous—a loss of peaceful,
faith-filled contentment.

you *and* me time

1. Begin a new family tradition—create a "blessing book." (Scrapbookers may enjoy embellishing this with their kids.) Use this book regularly or on special occasions (birthdays, Thanksgiving, etc.) to remember all the ways God has met your needs as a family.

2. Talk to your children about a character in one of their favorite children's books or movies (one with a happy ending). What does that character feel in the middle of the story when he or she doesn't know what's going to happen? But your children know what happens at the end, don't they? Talk about it. What's the end of the story?

   Then share with your kids a time when you had to wait on the Lord—you might still be waiting—and what that felt like: the emotions you went through and the questions you asked God. But explain that God knows the end of your story, and the end of the story of the world, and He has great plans that you don't know about. Read your children the verses that have brought you comfort when you were waiting. Then ask them if there is something for which they are waiting and trusting, and pray together for contentment in waiting for God's timing and trusting His understanding of all time.

live *it* out

1. Get in the habit of regularly thanking God aloud for various gifts of His throughout the day—a shade tree, air-conditioning, or cold water on a hot day; money to buy groceries; a safe neighborhood. This can help your family develop an "attitude of gratitude."

2. Verbally differentiate between things you "want" and things you "need."

3. Honestly, prayerfully consider the things you, as a parent, are fearful of. How are you communicating those fears to your children? Pray that God would cause you to choose faith and to impart that faith to your kids.

contentment

OBSERVATIONS, PRAYERS, AND ANSWERS

endurance

WITHSTANDING LASTING DIFFICULTY

God only comes to those who ask him to come; and he cannot refuse to come to those who implore him long, often, and ardently.

—SIMONE WEIL

endurance DAY ONE

[What is to come] calls for patient endurance
on the part of the saints who obey God's
commandments and remain faithful to Jesus.
—REVELATION 14:12 (NIV)

PRAYER FOCUS

Dear God, may Your Holy Spirit encourage _____ to begin building a lifestyle of patient endurance. Instill in _____ a willingness to obey Your commandments and always be faithful to Jesus Christ. Deepen his trust in You as his God and Savior.

Then Nebuchadnezzar said, "Praise be to the God of Shadrach, Meshach and Abed-nego, who has sent his angel and rescued his servants! They trusted in him and defied the king's command and were willing to give up their lives rather than serve or worship any god except their own God." —DANIEL 3:28 (NIV)

PRAYER FOCUS

Lord, how I pray that my child would develop a heart of endurance like these young men, Shadrach, Meshach, and Abednego. Give _____ the strength to stand firm when facing adversity. Help him to say, "I serve God, and He is able to save me from any situation. But even if He doesn't, I will not disobey Him; I will do what I know is right in His sight."

Endurance requires a lifestyle built on trusting
God and being obedient to Him.

endurance DAY TWO

*Blessed is the man who perseveres under trial, because
when he has stood the test, he will receive the crown
of life that God has promised to those who love him.*
—James 1:12 (NIV)

PRAYER FOCUS

Father, thank You that You will never leave us or forsake us. As _____
faces difficult situations, remind her of this truth. Strengthen her to endure
these trials so that one day she can receive the crown of life You promised to
those who love You.

*It is commendable if a man bears up under the pain of unjust suffering because he is
conscious of God. But how is it to your credit if you receive a beating for doing wrong
and endure it? But if you suffer for doing good and you endure it, this is commendable
before God.* —1 Peter 2:19–20 (NIV)

PRAYER FOCUS

Father, there are so many difficult things my child must face in these days. I ask
that _____ would be a young person who will have the strength and
courage to stand up under these pressures because she is striving to live for You.
Allow _____ to recognize that she might have to suffer for doing
what she knows is right, but that through her endurance, her actions will be
pleasing to You.

PERSONAL PRAYER

Pray for your child's faithfulness in the adversity and pressures she is enduring
right now.

*Endurance is the capacity to bear up under difficult,
unpleasant, painful, stressful circumstances—
in a Christlike manner.*

endurance DAY THREE

Those enduring to the end shall be saved.
—MATTHEW 24:13 (TLB)

PRAYER FOCUS

Father, I know that as a believer in Jesus Christ, my child will have to expect and face persecution for his faith. Please sustain him with Your presence. Supply _____ with the endurance he needs to stand firm against all opposition.

Everyone will hate you because you are mine. But all who endure to the end without renouncing me shall be saved. —MARK 13:13 (TLB)

PRAYER FOCUS

Dear God, when _____ 's faith is challenged, stand by him as he learns to endure these attacks. I pray that he will become even stronger in his faith in You.

PERSONAL PRAYER

Pray for God's strength in those aspects of your child's faith that are particularly vulnerable to attack—and in persecution that would be especially discouraging to him.

Endurance is essential to faith.

endurance DAY FOUR

Let us not get tired of doing what is right, for after a while we will
reap a harvest of blessing if we don't get discouraged and give up.
—GALATIANS 6:9 (TLB)

PRAYER FOCUS

Father, I pray that You would gently build endurance into _____'s
life. Give _____ a heart that helps her to keep on pressing on even
when she faces discouragement and is tempted to give up.

Therefore, since we are surrounded by such a great cloud of witnesses, let us throw off
everything that hinders and the sin that so easily entangles, and let us run with perse-
verance the race marked out for us. —HEBREWS 12:1 (NIV)

PRAYER FOCUS

Lord, You have sovereignly marked our path. I ask that You would enable
_____ to run the race of life with great endurance. Keep
_____ from being tripped up, distracted, or discouraged in the
race. Help her to keep her eyes on You.

PERSONAL PRAYER

Pray for wisdom—and courage—to lovingly build endurance into your child's
life.

Endurance is the patient, committed pursuit
of those things that please God.

endurance DAY FIVE

No temptation has overtaken you but such as is common to man;
and God is faithful, who will not allow you to be tempted beyond
what you are able, but with the temptation will provide the way of
escape also, so that you may be able to endure it.
—1 Corinthians 10:13 (NASB)

PRAYER FOCUS

Lord, give _____ the endurance to stand against every temptation.
Deliver _____ from ever giving up on looking to You for strength,
wisdom, and encouragement.

You have need of endurance, so that when you have done the will of God, you may
receive what was promised. . . . But my righteous one shall live by faith; and if he
shrinks back, my soul has no pleasure in him. But we are not of those who shrink back
to destruction, but of those who have faith to the preserving of the soul. —Hebrews
10:36, 38–39 (NASB)

PRAYER FOCUS

Father, please give _____ a spirit of endurance. Build him up so that
he will not shrink back from a life of faith. Encourage him to not give up when
he encounters people or ideas that test his faith. I want _____ to
have the kind of faith that will preserve his soul.

Giving up can cause guilt and disappointment,
which take our focus off the Lord,
but a spirit of endurance keeps our eyes
on God and His purposes.

you *and* me time

1. To show how Christians sometimes must endure persecution for their beliefs, plan a mock trial in your home. Take turns as the judge, prosecutor, defendant, and defense counselor. Let the judge read the charges brought against the defendant. Here are some examples of possible charges:
   a. You believe that God created this world.
   b. You believe that the Lord is a personal God.
   c. You believe that Jesus Christ is God.
   d. You don't lie or cheat to get your own way.
   e. You avoid drugs, alcohol, and sex.

   Allow the prosecutor and defense counselor to take turns questioning and informing the defendant on the truth of the charges. Look up the following verses to see how one might biblically answer the charges. (Note: these verses correspond in order to the charges above.)
   a. Genesis 1–2; Psalm 19:1; Psalm 8:1–3; Romans 1:20
   b. Psalm 139; Jeremiah 9:24
   c. Colossians 1:15–17; John 1:1–2, 14
   d. Psalm 101:1–3; Psalm 15; Proverbs 6:16–19
   e. 1 Corinthians 6:18–20; Proverbs 23:26–32; Proverbs 7:6–27
2. With teenagers, read *Jesus Freaks* (dc Talk and the Voice of the Martyrs, 2002).

live *it* out

1. Set, plan out, and pursue a measurable, tangible goal with one of your children, or as a family, that will require a measure of endurance but will have a worthwhile reward. The goal may be physical ("Let's train for a 5K run together"), financial ("Let's save money for _____"), spiritual ("If we can all memorize [Scripture passage], we'll do [special activity] together"), or some other area.

endurance

OBSERVATIONS, PRAYERS, AND ANSWERS

appendix:
character-building
suggestions

1. When reading books or watching movies together, interact with your child about situations that arise or words that characters say. For younger children, ask about what a character may be feeling and what choices lie in front of that character. Before teaching your child, gently ask probing questions that will help your child discover the benefit of good character, problem-solve in a situation, and apply scriptural and moral principles.

2. In conversation—and in matters of discipline—examine the heart issues at stake rather than merely the outward "symptom" of a child's misbehavior. For example, if your child steals his or her sibling's granola bar, the situation extends beyond a swiped snack: you're dealing with issues of selfishness and a lack of love (or possibly revenge and anger if the child is retaliating because his or her own snack was stolen). Acknowledge your child's legitimate desire (i.e., wanting a snack) and his or her illegitimate choice, as well as what your child could have done differently. Ask heart-probing questions that lead your child to true repentance rather than just behavior modification (see Matthew 23:27–28). For more on this topic, consider Tedd Tripp's parenting classic *Shepherding Your Child's Heart* (FamilyLife.com).

3. Make character words common in your home, especially when you're affirming a particular character trait you see in your children, so that they can identify what these traits look like in their lives. Talk often about the qualities in this guide that you're praying for your children—and when you see answers to your prayers for a specific character trait you want to instill in your children, hug them and let them know that you've been praying for God to develop this quality in them, and you're proud of their wise choice.

4. As a family, memorize character-related scriptures together—and celebrate your achievements. For example, families with older children might memorize 1 Corinthians 13 together, and when everyone's succeeded, celebrate by going out to dinner.

5. Offer a special privilege to a child who's "caught having character"—a recurring award for a child showing extraordinary kindness, teachability, and so on, with consideration of each child's struggles and developmental abilities. Your child could get a special snack, be allowed to pick the movie for family movie night, or be temporarily relieved of a daily chore.

6. Talk about people you and your children know (or know of) who've exemplified character in real-life situations. Point out character that you see in your spouse or other relatives: "I'm so glad you have a dad who's responsible and takes care of our home and our yard." For examples from history, check out the Read-Aloud Stories for Families series by Barbara Rainey (FamilyLife.com).

about the authors

ANNE ARKINS is the mother of four grown children, grandmother to eleven, writer, and a Bible study leader in Bella Vista, Arkansas. She has a degree in secondary education from the University of Arkansas. Anne and her husband, Jim, also serve on FamilyLife's Weekend to Remember® speaker team.

GARY HARRELL is a teaching pastor at Fellowship Bible Church of Northwest Arkansas. He and his wife, Anne, have two grown daughters and five grandchildren. Gary graduated from the University of Arkansas with a degree in business administration, and also holds a Master of Theology degree from Dallas Theological Seminary, a Master of Christian Education from Southwestern Baptist Theological Seminary, and a Doctor of Ministry from Fuller Theological Seminary.

about FamilyLife

FamilyLife® is a donor-supported nonprofit organization headquartered in Little Rock, Arkansas, whose mission is to develop godly marriages and families who change the world one home at a time. Cofounded in 1976 by Dennis and Barbara Rainey, FamilyLife has strengthened millions of marriages and families through numerous resources, including:

- Weekend to Remember® marriage getaway
- The Art of Marriage® video marriage conference
- *FamilyLife Today*® and *Real FamilyLife*® *with Dennis Rainey* radio broadcasts
- HomeBuilders small-group studies
- LifeReady®—success training for today's marriages and families
- FamilyLife eMentoring™—one-to-one help and hope
- FamilyLife.com
- Hope for Orphans®

FamilyLife works in more than one hundred countries around the world and utilizes a volunteer network of more than ten thousand couples nationwide who help bring God's message to others through the practical application of time-tested techniques and teachings that are based on biblical principles.

Through the guidance of FamilyLife's experts and with the help of their lay ministry, FamilyLife has developed into a vibrant and visionary organization that is today changing the world one home at a time.